The Burning Alphabet

Also by Barry Dempster

POETRY:

Tributaries (1978, editor)
Fables for Isolated Men (1982)
Globe Doubts (1983)
Positions to Pray In (1989)
The Unavoidable Man (1990)
Letters from a Long Illness with the World: the D.H. Lawrence Poems (1993)
Fire and Brimstone (1997)
The Salvation of Desire (2000)
The Words Wanting Out: Poems Selected and New (2003)

FICTION

Real Places and Imaginary Men (1984, short stories)
David and the Daydreams (1985, children's fiction)
Writing Home (1989, short stories)
The Ascension of Jesse Rapture (1993, novel)

The Burning Alphabet

Barry Dempster

Brick Books

Library and Archives Canada Cataloguing in Publication

Dempster, Barry, 1952-
        The burning alphabet / Barry Dempster.

Poems.
ISBN 1-894078-42-X

I. Title.

PS8557.E4827B87 2005   C811'.54   C2005-900403-7

We acknowledge the support of the Canada Council for the Arts,
the Government of Canada through the Book Publishing Industry
Development Program (BPIDP), and the Ontario Arts Council for
their support of our publishing program.

   Canada

Cover art: Goodwin, Betty Roodish, Canadian, 1923
Moving Towards Fire, 1983. Oil, coloured chalks, graphite, water-
colour on thin wove paper. 291 x 108 cm. (each sheet); 291 x 324 cm.
(installed). Art Gallery of Ontario, Toronto. Purchase, 1985.
With the permission of Galérie René Blouin, Montréal.

The author's photograph is by Glenn Hayes.

The book is set in American Typewriter, Minion and Officina Sans.

Design and layout by Alan Siu.

Printed by Sunville Printco Inc.

Brick Books
431 Boler Road, Box 20081
London, Ontario N6K 4G6
www.brickbooks.ca

30 Years Young
Brick Books 1975–2005

For Karen

Contents

ANGEL HUSKY

EXPLICIT

Above all, I cherish the explicit:

the green light at the corner
of now and then; the thrust of words
like *grab* and *shout*; the alphabetical
listings – *albatross, breast, cuneiform*
in *The Dictionary of Dreams.*

In the haze of momentary lapses
I reach for the nearest doorknob.
Coasting the tap from hot to cold.
Such confidence: flicking a switch,
unbuttoning your buttons, expelling a verb.

Even mystery has its sure
things: snakes slithering into new
skins, the closed-closet taste of Brussel
sprouts, abandoned golf balls on the moon.

How perfect those hole-in-one philosophies,
the bluntness of lotteries, the unerring
aim of flash floods, viruses,
missiles of lightning – the moment
gone straight to fate.

It's only the forgotten or
the never tried who suddenly
die, tripping over an end table,
falling from a window that looked
just like a work of art. It's those who
don't know how many cigarettes
they've smoked, those who lose themselves
in daydreams of some special place,
those who love the ambiguity

of their deepest feelings, they're the ones
who quietly dissolve.

The trick is: definitive, stunning
things like *brandy, fluorescence, arias,
the hammer of red and blue.*

Tie it all into knots: fists and
clots and first impressions, life
at its most infallible.

Feel each finger as it creates
a hand, each heartbeat billowing
a Niagara of the blood, each
thought a circle so round
it makes the moon look slack.

HANDPRINTS

After half-an-hour's dusty drive from Los Alamos,
and another half-hour climb up a hot cliff
I found myself scrunched inside
a cave the size of a child's playhouse,
surprisingly warm and damp
as if corpses had started to breathe again.
Paintings on the slippery walls –
square horses, empty circles,
men made of burnt sticks.
And there beside me
a crinkled handprint, fingers spread.

Touch me, I said out loud
startling the miniature echoes
from their long stupors.
My palm and the rock both sweating,
I leaned forward, my flesh
doubling its hardness, smacking
against the wall, shattering
each small grain of loneliness.
Someone long ago touched me back.

Here and now, huddled
in what little is left of Ontario's fall
I stand by the living room window
palm prints smearing cool grey glass,
a kind of braille. *Touch me:*
as if someone might actually
drive down this street, make the long
climb out of their warm car
to reach me, lifelines mingling.

Is that a human being
at the window across the street
or just a stick of furniture
pressed too close to an empty curtain?
Over here, I wave, all those years of me

gathering into one small act.
After a lonely day, I lay a hard hand
on the place where my heart
chisels away at rock.
This fumbled stroke, another
smudge lost in the blur.

THE DEAD ELM

In certain moonlight, the dead elm
is Kabuki, bark the colour
of a wet ghost, branches flourishing
shadows like sleeves, a creature
towering over my small roof
and measly chimney. How easy to
crush me in the middle of the night
when my good dreams and bad dreams
are symbols of unlived life.

Take it down, my nervous friends
advise, *call the tree mortician.*
Okay, I think, let rabid bats hang
upside down in someone else's brain.
I'll watch as all the stranded cats,
the ones with rheumy eyes and ripped ears,
tear fallen sparrows' nests to shreds.
Shouts of *Timber* like a heart surgeon's
thumps, as the old fellow loses
limb after limb. I picture
those neat Stonehenge piles of
firewood bleached bone by the sun.

But would I truly be safe
with the dead elm tumbled down and
just the sky above me, the voice of
Chicken Little ringing in my ears?
People die in their sleep, untouched,
airplanes crashing out of nowhere,
no survivors in the end.
The tree and I, we keep track
of one another's rot, neither
living nor dying alone, sharing
the paleness of midnight when
the grass is sound asleep and the ants
are inventing the miniature wheel.

WHEN THE GODS DON'T LOVE YOU

On the day Clytie declassified
the contents of her heart
she lay down in the dirt,
dew-smeared, her toes digging
ten diminutive graves.

The romantics claim
she turned into a sunflower,
her will to live collapsing
into soft golden heaps.

Hope shut down, disappointment
curled in the blackness of her breast
like a dead seed. It would have been
wiser to have loved herself
instead of faithless Apollo,
embracing her own shadow
as it climbed the garden wall.

When I realized that none
of the gods loved me either,
I simply dusted off my desire
to die and went inside.

I lit a fire in the first available emptiness,
arranged a bit of comfort
to go with the warmth, curtains and mirrors,
all the choices I could imagine,
all the details someone else might neglect.
Instead of flowers in a vase, I set out
a display of bones, tiny white ones
picked from the fist of my heart.

A SMALL JUNGLE

Despite those dapper pink and green spikes
the dracaena looks edgy
in its flimsy plastic pot,
the lonely anxiety of the too tall.
So I add an asparagus fern
to my flourishing shopping cart.
Not truly belonging to the fern family
it greets the dracaena
all tendrils and want.

Past the pomp of hibiscus blooms
and rows and rows of fledgling poinsettias,
I spot my next purchase,
a straggly spider plant
gesturing everywhere, to no-one.
Lastly, a sturdy terra-cotta pot
large enough for everything.
We will all live together, a small jungle.

What I'm longing for is family,
not the one I've got, not the mother
wilting away from lack of memory,
not father with his touch-mc-nots of misery,
not the only child make-believe
of bigger brothers or *Little Shop of Horror* pets,
but constellations, encyclopedias,
English gardens competing for light,
for blossoms and shrubbery, somewhere
I can squeeze into the thick of belonging.

DETACHED

This morning, as every morning,
the a.m. shows stunned me
with their peculiar shade of hope,
people in the prime of their desires.
I want to be king,
said a man up for public office,
at least his eyes said so,
shimmering blue crowns.
To be a star,
echoed an actress in a supporting role.
Want upon want, layers of it
like a high-rise box of chocolates.
To be happy, crooned a model,
a brand name floating across her face.

Just because my wants are off-camera
doesn't mean I'm satisfied.
Unprotected from those garish TV rays
my skin goes pink,
a squirmy sort of colour
clashing with everything I wear or think.
In the shower I'm suddenly gripped
by an overwhelming wish
to be someone else.
I want to be a mogul, or an astronaut,
I sputter at the God of Seldom There.

A little someone lives inside of me
who will never be invited on an a.m. show.
Every now and then he feels like friction,
sandpaper rubbed against my heart.
Other times, he's so quiet,
we don't feel much of anything.

ANGEL HUSKY

For ten minutes yesterday
I was cosmically loved, not
by some vision of smoke-thin wrists
curling in the November mist,
not from a memory blown in my face
in a puff of witch-doctor dust,
not even from one of those I-feel-
like-the-last-man-on-earth encounters
with God. No, it was a simple
out-of-bounds, a sticky flurry of
sopping leaves, a sudden leap:
one blue eye, one gold, dividing
me into soul and precious body.

It looked like Siberian Husky,
though it thundered like a waterfall,
soaking me with approval,
circling until I was ringed with
afterglow, my jeans streaked with paw-print
comets. If ghosts had tongues like
post-coital penises, then that pounce
of wet fur was a four-star phantom.
There was nothing I could do but
open my arms, like hugging a
cosmic flood, holding nothing back.

Ten minutes of total acceptance:
a snout in my beard, a tail thumping
against my flesh, a quiver of
whiskers melting in my ears.
Not a thought to what diseases
we might be sharing. No need for
Certs or a spurt of cologne.
It took me as I was, excited
by the gasp of my energy,

the space in the mist I'd made for
myself, the spot on the street where
my shadow and I folded into a shield.

If *Genesis* had taken the trouble
to explain how God made streams,
it would have gone something like this:
a giant tongue and a willing surface.
Feeling like the world was about
to begin again, *après* flood,
I stood there, arms outstretched,
blissfully embracing the mist.

DEER

Amidst the cushy sole prints of *Nikes*
and the pussy-willow pads of pampered
terriers and labs, a sudden set of
deer tracks, a seashell stamp of hooves.
So close to backyard patios, the
chorus lines of marigolds look bruised,
the lawns tousled, a window or two smeared.
In the thick of night, when we're dreaming of
corridors and Dali clocks, the soft brown
bodies of bucks and does are basking
in our moonlight, nibbling on the last of our
lettuce leaves, scratching impressions in our sand.
They are the children we wish we'd had,
fleeting images of ourselves before
inner lives grew blotchy, eyes heavy with
10 p.m. cop shows and those blessedly
nonsensical dreams. They are shadows
of joy and appetite, marauders of
starlight, property of instinct and whim.

Occasional Fridays or Saturdays
we tiptoe outside at midnight, wishing
we could sneak a smoke or feel up someone
behind the bushes. Longing to be wanton,
even irresponsible. Tear some
turf, rip a zinnia, devour
a handful of fireflies. Although,
touching a deer would do, stroking that muscled
satin, drinking from its black-coffee eyes.
Leaving a bare footprint next to a pair of
hooves. Here we are, stroking
the invisible, stamping our feet
through the flower beds, fools doing the
Twist or Frug, the sand between our toes
slowly turning to mud in the dew.

Face it, we no longer belong out here.
Moonlight hurts, like mercury searing

nerves and tissue. We only have
a minute, calling in the cats, before
we start mistaking every shadow
for something we shouldn't desire.
Slam those doors, snap those chains, curtains keep us
safely 60 watt. How much later is it
before our yards are filled with deer, raccoons,
foxes, unicorns? We'll never know,
we've already disappeared. Tomorrow,
sun struck, eager to weed or hold a hose,
we'll notice the tracks again, those spilled grains
of sand. *Deer*, we'll whisper, an endearment,
being gentle with our lost, imagined selves.

UNBELIEVABLE, AN OCTOBER POEM

When it comes, spring will be
unbelievable. Where did those
dolled-up irises find their purple
robes? That sweetly pissy smell
of dandelions, suddenly airborne.
And all the forget-me-nots,
just a pale haze of blue,
like someone in the desert
imagining a backyard pool.
Spring was made to be doubted,
a god drawn in edible crayons,
a spiderweb for a head, snare
of fingers teased over the earth like roots.

Painful thoughts for October. What
about that old man parked on the bench
having his fingers sniffed by hungry
squirrels? Was he ever young and
purple? Today it is cold. Springless.
Fallen leaves forget their stems
before they hit the ground.

I take hold of my suburban
machete, cutting down the brittle
garden. Close to the ground, the day
is brown, piles of it, dogshit
and nutshells and broken branches.
It feels like I've been doing this
forever. But then my wife, her hands
dressed up in dirty cotton gloves,
says something about next year,
the coreopsis taking over,
the swelled head of the silver mound,
the yarrow with its feathery fear
of heights, and I'm speechless at how
little I remember dirt.
The tulip bulb in my fingers
is only an onion gone wrong.

CLOSET

A dim grey day until my wife
swings open her closet doors
and the sway of a thousand blossoms
startles the room, dresses
blooming haphazardly,
skirts cascading from hangers
like sprays of honeysuckle, blouses
bunched in shimmering bouquets.

I remember my mother's closet
with its hopscotch plaids and hushed pastels,
like a board game for Avon ladies.
A beige pair of polyester pants
rubbed up against a pink sweater
with buttons that shone like tiddlywinks.
Skirts woven from clumps of widows' hair.
A blue angora sweater
shedding like a nervous Pekingese.

What wonders transpire
in the closets of my female friends?
As a child, I pictured Sandra Dee
folding herself perfectly
in a tissue-paper-lined box.
Cousin Joan running
her long, red fingernails
through a rainbow of linen and silk.
Even a stranger's face
on a rainy day, a mist of
green eyes and plum-coloured scarf,
opens that closet door a crack.

I can sometimes be found
in my wife's closet
which is half-mine,

the giddy legality of marriage.
Fingering the surprisingly
silver roses of a party dress
I feel far beyond myself
(a mere man hanging laundry)
like Jason sealing his thumbprints
on the edges of the Golden Fleece.
This purple and scarlet
skirt of flying poppies
is more than just something
my wife likes to wear:
it's the way she dreams
when days are dim suits of armour
and frost has mussed her eyelashes
with crystals of grey air.

SEX, A WISH LIST

Dirty, I wanted it dirty
like the kind of things men did under cars
to make their faces wet and black,
or women when they
backed out of sweaty ovens
trickles of butter running down their necks.
In girlie magazines the models
were rose or cream
and tasted like empty paper plates,
crumpling, even tearing,
when they kissed.

Sorry Mom, this boy
isn't interested in good clean fun.
He wants smudges and snail smears
all the way down his naked chest,
his belly button full of spit,
grubby fingerprints on his penis.
Tongues swiped across his lips,
electric pools of bruises
shining in a dark tangle of thighs.

Filthy, I dreamt it was
filthy, a man at midnight
leaping into the mud puddle
of a bedroom door,
leaving nothing of himself outside.
I was hoping to fuck the earth
the way gods do, to throw my dust
in their lava, to be that flame.

HOW TO FORGET YOU

I will stare at the uncaring sun
until my eyes explode, memory
shattering into a million sparks.
The flash containing you
will rise above most of my other
illuminations, the flame whisked
into that great forgetfulness of blue.

I will wait until dusk, then
pour myself a tears and soda,
watch as all those weak and
sappy bubbles splash and burst.

I will peel all your pictures
from the glossy photo album
with the daisies on the cover.
Erase the guise of your name
from poetry books.
Boil the red from raspberries,
ban the vowels in *The Lord's Prayer*,
cut the cries from violins.
Remove any of my body parts
you might have touched.

I will clean out the old brain
attic, up to my elbows in
heartstrings and Cupid dust.
Toss out the chairs with broken backs,
the circular arguments
missing a spiral or two,
the promises with frazzled hems.
Rediscover that treasure,
the one thing I thought
I couldn't live without.
Bury it in the backyard, next to

the peony and its endless
stream of mourner ants.

I will simply never think
of you again, lift off my head
and carry it heavily
under my left arm like the globe
of an undiscovered planet.

STORMY WEATHER

At first the day's a leaky shower head
threads and threads of drizzle
sweat drooling down the back of my neck.
But then the skies begin crowding together
bench-pressed clouds
and a sudden torrent of rain
needing multi-syllables to do it justice.
Athabasca! Magnifique! Kakabeka!
White alyssum
exploding into silver aftershocks.
Rec rooms flooding
tasteless TV trays and horseshoe hassocks
drowned in one great gulp.
Asphalt rapids and drainpipe cascades.
The world before the world.

Damp, the weatherman moans
making the whole day
sound like kidney stones.
Where is his passion?
In Saigon, motorbikes
ride through the rainy season
like sailboats.
On the downpour streets of Aberdeen
everyone glistens
the way they do after sex.
Ah, *The Tempest*, the Flood
the sultry *Stormy Weather*
where shamans sweat-dance
with purple orchids
and a raven, mid-air, bursts
from the gleaming body of a dove.

Never mind *damp*, never mind
the headlines of taxes, the Conservative
leadership campaign, all

swept into sewers.
It's just me and the rain
thunder and bone
a man made entirely of beads
of sweat, pouring himself
down the windowpane, a deluge
a vision, the world reshaped.

ETCETERA

11 a.m., the day barely knee-high,
and I've already learned latex comes from
poppies as well as rubber trees, last night's
Tonys netted *The Producers* 12 noisy
awards, this will be the 13th straight day of
rain. Facts to live by, filling the empty
vases with energy, swelling the brain cells
into fuchsias and peonies. Alive!
Encore! An acceptance speech in
every raindrop. I am continued,
a shine on the colour grey, like paint boasting.

In the beginning God created the
interior monologue: *gee, I sure wish
there was light.* On and on, words teeming like
poppies. Let me count the days, the number
of lives I'd like to fill, the empty spots
wrinkles have yet to spill. There is nothing
more satisfying than asking myself
what I want for lunch, looking forward to
towering clouds blowing off their grey blooms,
breathing in the air I just breathed out.

Mañana... may it multiply, shimmer
and assume. Who knows what facts await:
caterpillars curing cancer, or
sudden peace on earth. More and more time for
never enough, as lists accumulate,
and longing grows taller than brains. I would
like to thank persistence for being there.
Without the number 14, none of this
would have been possible. Etcetera
rolls off the tongue like a drop of spun
energy casting ripples through the day.

MR. MEMORY

i.

Nostalgia is compulsive, oompahpah, ploughing
through scrolls and picture frames.
How many fancy restaurants?
Comets, leap years, parades?

But I seem to have lost my special occasions,
their buzz. Is that a blank stare on Prince Philip's face,
his right hand fixated on something as disconnected
as a glove, while his left rolls dead skin into a tiny ball?

Some of me is unforgettable: the gamy taste
of mushrooms from a can, the giddy
feel-me-ups of bubble envelopes, the fifth
Beatle hiss of an old 45.

But where have the ultras gone: the Rijks
Museum, the Falkland war, *The Nutcracker*?
How much of me have I managed to forget?

An old man, I can imagine him now, tasting
toast and honey no matter what he eats,
galvanized by one January, one shoelace, one glimpse.

Did I ever tell you about the antler
I found when I was just a boy? His eyes
dart over my unfamiliar face, like a deer
sizing up the moment, its head soft and bare.

ii.

How dare you leave these memories behind:
blue bike splayed against the sagging fence,
frisbees bolting over the pool like UFOs,
Ball of Confusion blasting rec room walls, Miss
Ass and the Virgin, bang of *Harvey's* pickles
on a Friday night. Just the nicknames alone
qualify for dead language status.
No wonder my heart keeps
sinking, snapshots piled upon keepsakes,
until the sum of us ends up in the soles of my feet.

Step by step, the earth forgets to hold me,
until I have no choice but to grab the blue
of that ancient bike and pedal myself
a decade or two, to the edge of the almost
forgotten pool where the past floats on its back
and can no longer tell the difference
between a frisbee and the moon.

Ball of Confusion is the best we could do.
Sitting in *Harvey's* on a Friday night,
making up names for all the women
who lost us long ago. Mr. Memory
and the Dead Guy. Behind every
blank stare is a brain brimming over.
How dare the fences fall. How
dare time lose its way in space.

SUBURBAN POET

8 a.m., suburban street
like an abandoned movie set.
Lawns looking fake with velvety grass
and fashionably thin lodgepole pines.
Basketball hoops in the driveways
filled with autumn leaves
like Martha Stewart centrefolds.
Front doors wreathed in bittersweet
and *White Rose* ribbons.
All the pumpkin-faced garbage bags smiling.

Perfection is how you describe it
off in your office towers
and factory lines.
Can't wait to get home
to rakes and vases
to those black poodles
prancing about the yard.
Light the *IKEA* lamp in the window
peer out into a close-up of the night
as it swings across the sky.

Ah, but you never should have let a poet in
lonely all those weekday mornings
nothing to do but describe.
Sure, he sings your praises
comes up with words like *velvety*
but deep inside he feels abandoned
like those autumn mums in the garden
showing off for no-one
now that Daylight Saving Time
has forced it dark by 6.

On Tuesday, aching just a little
around the heart
he uses the word *fake*
several times in the same line.
By Wednesday, the basketball hoops

are described as huge rats' nests.
Thursday, the bittersweet berries
are blood clots.
Friday, the garbage bags are leaking
dead leaves all over the street.

One night you drive home
exhausted by all the city's flaws
and find the poet naked
in your driveway, posed, ready
to piss on your tires.
His body is unfashionably pale
his penis like an unravelled ribbon.
Fake, he screams loudly.
You think of sewers and compost heaps
those unsightly necessities.

The second time
you actually grapple
get out the garden hose
and blast him.
By the fourth or fifth encounter
you're running him down with your mini-van.
Finally, you scream too –
words like *lovely* and *exquisite*
delighted by how quickly he shrivels
backing up into a nest of rakes.

All it will take now is an early snow
one of those paper weights you shake
until it turns into a blizzard
suffocating all that fall mess.
Come spring, the poet
will have almost decomposed
just a penis poking from the dirt
like the tip of a tulip bulb.
Velvety, you'll say, and *fake*
stroking it into full bloom.

SICK DAYS

Considering how common illness is, how
tremendous the spiritual change that it
brings, how astonishing, when the lights
of health go down, the undiscovered
countries that are then disclosed, what
wastes and deserts of the soul a slight
attack of influenza brings to view, what
precipices and lawns sprinkled with
bright flowers a little rise of temperature
reveals, what ancient and obdurate oaks
are uprooted in us by the act of sickness,
how we go down into the pit of death
and feel the waters of annihilation close
above our heads and wake thinking to
find ourselves in the presence of the
angels and the harpers when we have a
tooth out and come to the surface in the
dentist's armchair and confuse his 'Rinse
the mouth – rinse the mouth' with the
greeting of the Deity stooping from the
floor of Heaven to welcome us – when
we think of this, as we are so frequently
forced to think of it, it becomes strange
indeed that illness has not taken its
place with love and battle and jealousy
among the prime themes of literature.

Virginia Woolf

1/ Diagnosis

Everything but truth becomes loathed in a sick-room.
Harriet Martineau

Diagnosed and damned.
Ill – three mere letters
trying to look alike.
Thief of peace, the body
viciously disloyal.

∞

Illness is a thump, a shout,
face-first on the floor.
Doctors believe I'm being brave.
Minus my praise, God deems
I've simply stopped.

∞

Is there such a place
as illness, a planet hung
in all that space,
somewhere airless
where miracles go to grieve?

∞

Mind/body, the helpful exclaim:
mind of the blood, of the tear ducts,
mind of the nerves and kneecaps,
too much negative thinking, cells
slumped, even blood slipping into knots.

2/ After Reading Yet Another Article on Deadly Viruses

*If there is anything unhealthy in your reactions, just
bear in mind that sickness is the means by which an
organism frees itself from what is alien; so one must
simply help it to be sick, to have its whole sickness
and to break out with it.*

Rainer Maria Rilke

I picture small and dainty:
bite-sized tart, swirl of whipped cream
on top like a baker's hat.
Something I've gulped with pleasure,
something that made me lick my fingers.
Once it entered my system
the custard exploded from the
pastry, exposing, smaller still,
a trickle of spit, a gob of
alien plasma. This is
way beyond paranoia. Now
phlegmy little creatures slurp my cells.

Visualize: rows of killer
bacilli, faces ferret-like, slowly
sinking in slime, their soaking-wet
trench coats weighing them down. Drown,
I image. Drown. A spray of bubbles,
high-pitched hiss, a final *glub glub*.
One by one the viruses die,
angstroms of them, queasy aches
and fevered gypsy shivers,
leaving me roomy and relieved.

I'll never swallow again. Lick me
if you like but I won't lick back.
No way I'm hosting anything,
no farewell bashes, no dirty
doorknobs, no speck of bitterness
or envy. I take my fears to
that great copy shop in my head,
make a thousand replicas, a squad
of paper panic boats setting out
across the woozy mucus seas.

3/ Mother Nature

She had burst from the zoo of our dreams...
John Steffler

Beginning of August
yet a March-like wind
whips through the bedroom
wrinkling the Picasso, flattening
the philodendron against the wall.
Too weak to move, I am
buffeted and bruised, my
fever gulping down the cool.

There is nowhere
Mother Nature won't go
and nothing to which she will not stoop.
Unlike the grey-haired actress
selling margarine, the goddess
with water lilies on her breasts,
the homely nurse who lives only to serve,
she is wild with her own mutability,
a frenzied finger painting.

Shifting seasons, stirring sick rooms
into tempests, she is the same one
who sprouted this virus in me
and raised fleas on my cats,
who conceived the fabulous food chain
giving *National Geographic*
its slasher movie glare.

Ah, the little Brethren boy within me
sighs, *believe in her.*
The Loch Ness monster carries mysteries
in its small, bald head,
the Wild Man of China beats his chest

with legendary unreason, the holy
Abominable Snowman avoids us all.
Meanwhile, Mother Nature flourishes
here and now, growing moulds, mixing
hurricanes, pouring Petri dishes
down my cells. Hands on, she pummels
me, the immediacy of rapture.

When it feels like God
is toying with me from a distance
(*here's a panda bear, here's a coconut*)
Mother Nature is never further
than the bedroom window, taunting
me with gusts, with silverfish
and fleeting sexual *divertimenti*,
fevers and furies. Man amiss!
Man alive! Like little Fay Wray
in King Kong's fist.

4/ Signs of Health

In spite of illness, in spite even of the archenemy
sorrow, one can remain alive long past the usual date
of disintegration if one is unafraid of change,
insatiable in intellectual curiosity, interested in big
things, and happy in small ways.
                                        Edith Wharton

A rattly stethoscope, a steaming
vial of blood, my body
reduced to a list of symptoms.
Damaged immunity, the doctor

declares. I think murder trial,
electric chair. The red cells aren't
scheming with the white,
aren't doing their demanding jobs.

But life goes on with its marathons.
The chronically ill
learn to adjust their expectations,
hope behind glass: a dinosaur's egg.

A friend writes from Montreal
Margaret Atwood spotted on the steps
of *The Double Hook*.
On TV, Filipinos flee volcanoes

while Russians flock to cast their votes.
Just outside my window
a caramel cocker spaniel
sniffs absolutely everything.

If I could escape
I'd breathe it all:
Colorado, where the buttes and mesas
change shadows by the minute,

Mars with its ruddy bill of health,
a dot of green in the blue Caribbean,
a Greek bistro on the Danforth
where even the baklava has an appetite.

I'd wriggle out of these
cramped cells, this vial of dependable pain,
sail across my lawn,
green-bellied, whole again.

We are healed of a suffering only
by expressing it to the full.
Marcel Proust

5/ In Camera

Here, then, at last, is the definition of the image, of
any image: that from which I am excluded.
Roland Barthes

Here I am swallowing a camera
(to be said with voice pitched high
in disbelief). Or, to be more precise
(and blasé), swallowing an endoscope,
something to do with fibre optics
and awe. It goes down like a pony,
hooves digging into the crevices
where my tonsils used to be,
one gargantuan gulp. Of course,
as with most of life's big, bizarre moments,
I can't see myself curled on the stretcher
like an appliance plugged into a
nearby wall. There are no photos
of my Adam's apple lighting up,
my eyes rolling back into my head.

On the TV screen, as close up as
Baywatch cleavage: the inside of me.
Sesame Street would call it a tummy,
spelling out words like *rosy* and *rumbly*,
the gruesomeness of being human
transformed into cartoons. The doctor,
terminally afraid of feelings, labels it (me)
the lining of a gut, creating images of fish
and courage. The right word fails me:
belly, stomach, maw. I've never even
imagined it in the mirror before, this
conch shell occupant stretching
and squirming like a porn star.

This is, apparently, a picture of
the secret me, all muscle and mindlessness.

If I pinch my imagination just a bit,
the duodenum looks like a New Year's Eve
party hat. And here I thought I was all alone,
a phantom pain floating through all
the x-ray machines in the world. This must
be a picture of my deepest self, primitive
but companionable, sharing everything from
anxiety to Chinese food. As the camera
pulls out of me (a Walter Cronkite tone),
the cord slithering across my trachea
like a caterpillar, the screen begins
to blur, a deep red haze, a sunset
streaking by the windows of an airplane
as it climbs the clouds. Static, then
the glossy grey of a blank TV and
a reflection of my face, supremely
stunned. *I want to be a camera,*
I whisper (Garbo-like).

6/ Love Life

Everything in life that we really accept undergoes a change. So suffering must become Love. That is the mystery.
                                    Katherine Mansfield

Love life, cries the medical show
whose viewers are paralyzed
by torrents of adrenalin
as they discover how unfaithful
their hearts can be. Fibrillations,
irregularities, full arrests:
the multi-syllables of wills
and divorce decrees. Flesh puckers
at the ooze of an incision,
nipples collapsing as a chest
folds in two. The heart,
beefy and insensitive, skitters
in the surgeon's hands. 2 cc's
of lidocaine, a shock of paddles,
a good old-fashioned thump, any
violence, any indignity,
as long as the sucker keeps
quivering, the muscles grinding,
the blood roaring in and out.
This is it, life in a lump:
crude impossible pump.

7/ The Good Old Fears

What we feel and think and are is to a great extent
determined by the state of our ductless glands and viscera.
Aldous Huxley

Under your bed, bogeyman, flat,
furry backed, sucking on mattress springs.
Uncle Caveman swore he was
a smooth, saber-toothed tiger,
whiskers dripping blood. He's even
been Satan, smoky slashed tail,
dribbling lighter fluid down your neck.

How much we miss vampires,
anacondas, Godzilla
making matchsticks of Tokyo.
How often we long for the sky
to suddenly fall.

But this is a new millennium, all the monsters
speaking in rhymes in great glossy
children's books. What are you afraid of now?
Deer tick mistaking you for Bambi?
Mosquito bulging like a bag
of your own blood? A little bodily fluid?

Words veering in and out of fear. Ebola,
used to be some lovely little girl's name.
HIV, a brand of cherry pop. Wasn't it
Hepatitis who slew the crocodile
and saved all of Florida from
counterfeit tears? You can almost
remember those winters skiing
the slopes at Alzheimers, if only
your brain didn't feel like a frozen
bag of peas at the bottom of the hill.

Illness is the night-side of life, a
more onerous citizenship. Everyone
who is born holds dual citizenship,
in the kingdom of the well and in
the kingdom of the sick. Although
we all prefer to use only the good
passport, sooner or later each of us
is obliged, at least for a spell, to
identify ourselves as citizens of
that other place.

Susan Sontag

8/ Guardian Angels

There is, let us confess it (and illness is the great
confessional), a childish outspokenness in illness;
things are said, truths blurted out, which the cautious
respectability of health conceals.
                                        Virginia Woolf

I collect angels
the way some people have a drawerful
of St. Jude cards or rabbits' feet.
Surrounded by wings
of all shapes and sizes
        (widespread, flopping,
        folded into the spine like fortunes
        into Chinese cookies)
I may as well be living
in the firmament,
a paper match amongst
flocks of million-watt stars.

There is no way to be alone in my house.
Dominations of brass, wood and
other alternatives to flesh
fly back and forth across the walls.
Cherubim peer down from all the shelves,
dimples disguising their intensity.
An archangel the size of a six-year-old child
hangs mid-blessing in the bedroom.
Even the bathroom is immortal
with its seraphim-head soaps.

Waking up at night
from a dream of doctors
sawing off my wrists,
the house is humming with
guardian angels, whole choirs

of them, thrones and principalities,
diving through the darkness of my bed.
My shivers feel like feathers
plunged in every pore.
Wingspan! Breath pours out of me
as I rediscover my hands:
ten wide-awake fingers
clutching the hem of an angel
who is pretending to be made of wood.

9/ Sick Days

If you start to think about your physical or moral
condition, you usually find that you are sick.
                              Goethe

A valve in the sky gets stuck
and cold air spills in, strangling
the trees in their green nakedness.
Each blossom of the foxglove
freezes like a finger. Hummingbirds
leave little skid marks of breath.

∞

Someone is sick, a seasonal bug,
one of those airborne viruses from
Texas or Hong Kong, a sci-fi shock.
A case of shivers, a feverish dream
of cursing bones, their joints
flapping open like mouths.

∞

Strange: the sickness makes
its usual rounds – the nose, chest and
belly – only to start up all over again.
Symptoms in a panic, like wasps trapped
between windowpanes. Anemia, mono,
AIDS: a list as ruthless as an IQ test.
What super-secret virus eats up energy
and emits exhaust: hands so tired
they barely cast reflections on the sheets.

∞

Patience in a perpetual blur, a faint
thrumming, heaps of wellness
hollowed out, buckets filled with quicksand.
There goes hope, there goes tomorrow's plan,
a sip of water turned into a drip of sweat.
The word *chronic* sounds like it belongs
inside an engine. *Incurable*
is more exotic, memories lost in Marrakesh.

∞

Somebody, a fatherly tone of voice, dark
and unsure of himself, whispers *death*.

∞

Each molecule of the body
is responsible for itself. One sick thought
and ! suicide, negativity with its
tiny pricks of cyanide.

∞

Who would look here, a place
so bustled with immune cells, DNA's
been scrambled into SNAFU.
The end begins, an unexpected split, a
shopping cart collision. Disguised as
a ripple in the bowel or a microchip
in the brain, death counts down the days

with dry coughs and cramps
until it discovers the roominess of disease,
spreading from all directions like an octopus.

∞

Clamour of stethoscopes
against breastbones, crinkling of
blood-pressure cuffs cutting into upper arms,
crisp of needles piercing skin,
rumble of doctors as they pronounce
and condemn, sickness so loud
eardrums cower, nerves bristle
like whiskers, every sigh an assault.

∞

The only voice is the voice inside the head:
all loss and loneliness. God's voice
demanding a raise, or Buddha's
explaining this isn't nothingness yet.
The voice of the Body: factory squeal of
overworked machines and tools
falling on concrete floors. Enemy voice,
like voodoo pins. The voice of how it is,
nothing less, nothing more,
leaves rotting, skies spoiling,
time slicing eternity into bacon bits.

∞

Pain in the solar plexus, rage booming
its misery, a horror movie fetus
kicking flesh to kingdom come, kicking
holes in everything.

∞

Someone is always spooked at words
like *bedridden* and *invalid*, shunning them
like the witch-queen's dead-on mirror.
All illness is catching, from warts to wasting.
Just a glimpse of pale, pursed lips or frail pyjamas
and the mind prepares to faint, the body
abandoned to its fate.

∞

Sickrooms smell like Easter lily bulbs
just before they're stuffed in the dirt, that
nether world where moles, like velvet, undulate
and roots come equipped with ESP.
Bye-bye coffee, baseball gloves, money, adios
cinnamon, cut grass, glossy magazines,
adieu sex, asparagus, red wine in
plastic glasses, all illusions of self.

∞

The wisecracks ultimately flop
and self-pity explodes with the feeblest
of pops, and there's nothing there
but unease. Muscles ache, throat
sore, head woozy: identification marks.
It's the distance from the rest of the world
that makes these sick days endless,
miles and miles of loss, mountain ranges
lonely as sociopaths; serum, saliva
and blood in deep unswimmable seas.

10/ Getting Out of Bed

*Sickness comes to us all, Mr. Dillon.... We never know
when, we never know why, we never know how. The
only blessed thing we know is it'll come at the most
inconvenient, unexpected time. Just when you've got
tickets to the World Series. And that's the way the
permanent waves.*

Donald Westlake

All the morning intentions
overflowing the brain like a tub:
if I leap I'll bump my head
pain launched to the galaxy,
if I slide barefoot
the nails in the hardwood floor
are sparks of ice.
So I remain, pillow up my nose
snuggled in my own body heat
oblivious as a cat.

(The consequence of staying put
is watching the future
pull away from the curb
with a belch of coffee cream
a bad dream sneering
from the back window.)

Who should I be today?
Man with a briefcase, mustard and
relish, the tie with a thousand eyes?
Bum rolling through the gutters
like a huge dead leaf
from a prehistoric tree?
Frightened little boy
with a key on a string around his neck?

Flex those inchworms
of decision, the road behind
waving its ribbons of dirt.

And so the sleep-damp tunnel of me
(shedding skin), rolls off
the edge of the bed, a pile of
nakedness steaming on the floor.

No way of knowing what will happen next:
squirm, slither, explosion.
A stretch of a man, waking the air.

11/ Monet's Garden

A garden is not what you think...
Elizabeth Philips

Bad day, fevered, queasiness
running the length of my body
like long wet spider threads.
I imagine being back
in Giverny, bending over
a Japanese peony
breathing out instead of in,
dying into pale red folds. It's

a June day, yellow and buzzing,
with a faint whiff of pike
rising off the water lilies.
Bent over that peony, feeling
small like Toulouse-Lautrec,
his nose buried in a dancer's skirts.

From the vantage point of a bee
I'm a surrealist
in an impressionist garden.
The lime trees across the way
are relieved they don't
have to give bloom to me.
And the sky is the last blank page
in a coffee table art book.

A sick man means squat
in Monet's garden:
petal dropped
                petal lost.

p.s. colourful as it may seem
        this is an example
        of negative thinking, a waste
        of technicolour and sweat

better to dream about jesus
jumping out of a birthday cake
or someone named veronica
swallowing my house keys

imagine

if i'd been feeling positive
picasso and his blue machete
would have wrecked the place
all those self-pitying flowers
severed from their stems

Show him death, and he'll
be content with fever.
Persian Proverb

12/ Maple Fever

Our own physical body possesses a wisdom which we
who inhabit the body lack. We give it orders which
make no sense.
                    Henry Miller

3 a.m., when the chain link fence
is busy blowing bubbles with the dew
and wind chimes are humming
nursery rhymes to curious raccoons,
the maple outside my bedroom window
is turning red with pain, roots cramped,
branches tangled in a clutch.

My own insides
huddle around a ring of fever
like loyal boy scouts
bewitched by campfire flames.
I dream the pain slices right through me
as moonbeams watch from the window
and the maple stands and sways, hurting.

In the morning I'm weak,
nerves whispering that they have
something inconsequential to say.
Safely out of touch with the unseen
on this timid October day.
Until I whisk open the curtains
and am blinded by the tree, a red
piercing grimace. Exactly
how an ulcer might dream.

Ah, the Sunday drivers say, *look*
at the colour of these dying trees.
Gorgeous disease.

Bundling myself in appropriate
seasonal armour, I keep misery busy,
raking leaves into mounds, shovelling
soil, snapping broken branches
until my palms are scraped
bedsore raw, until I feel like Adam
after the trees had whipped him
with their long strips of bark.

13/ The Moment

Separation penetrates the disappearing person like
a pigment and steeps him in gentle radiance.
Walter Benjamin

4 p.m., Oprah Winfrey's empathy
haloing my easy chair
where I sit, statistic: white,
inner-child-abused male
in mid-life shock, watching October

blunt its crayons in the front yard,
oak leaves dying slower than
the maples, breezes breaking their falls,
streetlights waiting in the wings
for the launch of standard time.

Press of my ass against the pillow,
what is known as a quiet moment
with the self. Counting heartbeats the way
Oprah tallies up applause. *Men*
Who Worry About Everything.

Bathed in all the compassion of
last light, I am ready to confess
to the day that never really began,
the moment that is, but isn't,
a puddle slithering in search of a drain.

For an instant, I think I hear the anxious
drip of gastric juices. But it's only
a *Pepsi* commercial, beads of
October bronze falling down the throats
of celebrities, filling them with glow.

14/ Chill

Dead, one is not even alone any longer.
Elias Canetti

I read about D.H. Lawrence
counting his fears the way
a chiropractor rhymes off bones.
That trusty bugaboo of poverty,
stale bread dipped in a puddle moon.
War, and more war.
The slap of censorship, adultery,
damaging reviews.
Consumption
with its awesome army of red ants.
The dream not ever coming true.

I am afraid poems never say
enough, words cheating me
of rage, of passion.
The entire history of the planet
huddled in a panic attack.
Post-modern homelessness, cardboard soup.
Kuwaiti smoke, Chernobyl lesions,
Ethiopian banquets of blood.
The woman next door, nervous
for her unborn baby
who feels like a fatal wound.
My cousin who may or
may not be dying of AIDS,
desire with its Freddy Krueger *Boo!*

Last night, a rerun of the *X-Files*,
the ruthlessness of the dead's blind blue
eyes, the alien inside everyone.
Agent Mulder, like a snakebitten Christ.

Linear terror: can't trust purity,
good intentions, or even TV.
Can't count on luck or courage
to overcome us.
All I can cling to is hardcover DHL,
a life long lost, the faithful chill of ashes.

15/ Making Love to a Sick Man

You weep tears of health, of the onion, of the bee, of
the burning alphabet.

Pablo Neruda

The first thing you have to do
before making love to a sick man
is hold one of those compact mirrors
beneath his nostrils
and watch for swirls of mist.
If he's alive and ready,
you should be able to draw
a heart on the glass with your fingertip.

Proceed according to
the declarations of disease,
preparing him with condoms, paper
bags and ten foot poles, whatever
it takes to protect yourself.
Puffs of cotton in your ears are
recommended in case passion releases
one of his negative thoughts.

But by all means enjoy the surfaces.
A sick man's skin is unusually
soft. Bury your lips in his collarbones,
like grazing candy floss. Sink your
nipples into the wax pools of his eyelids.
Even his penis is fleecy,
like one of those lucky crystals
nestled in a blue velvet bag.

When you come, come
as if you were leaving
on a trip around the world,
dashing up a gangplank

or strapping on a pair of wings.
Coming and going
are synonymous to a sick man
as he lies there like a silk scarf
watching you zip and hook
your way back to the kingdom of health.
Everything beyond his bed
is an exit, so make it dramatic, make
it memorable. Blow him a kiss
that burns down the distance like a comet,
a streak of universe lighting up his eyes.

16/ New World

*In a sense sickness is a place, more instructive than
a long trip to Europe, and it's always a place where
there's no company, where nobody can follow.*
                                 Flannery O'Connor

Grim nights, propped up on three pillows,
banging my knees to distract myself,
the empty can thumps of my heart,
wondering whether I'll outlive my fear of dying.
Cries and crashes of the storm outside,
my backyard being dismantled:
the Mediterranean-blue shed
stripped board by board, oak branches
popped out like artificial limbs, blades
of grass butchered, roof tiles
ripped like bandages from hairy skin.
Close my aching eyes and picture
all three of my cats slinking across
the startled debris, padding on air, their tails
puffed up like homemade wings.

When the world is finally taken away
I'll miss the view, the fringed blind
snapped open, lace curtains shimmering
on lilac leaves as dark as ivy, and finches
the colour of whole wheat toast.
Mosquitoes stuck to the screen in
kamikaze frenzy; traffic, flatbeds full
of Holland Marsh carrots and onions;
hydro lines bulging against dusk skies
like body builder's veins; squirrels leaping
pine to pine, pretending to be crows.

Does illness make the world more precious,
or simply more obvious? The seen deconstructs
itself, busy suffering what was and will.
Daily, descriptions disappear, a leaf here,
a gloom there, hills eroding, creeks
condensing, even the darkness of grim nights
changing colours like a bruise. No wonder
morning feels like a new world, my fever
overpowered by the maze of sun through lace,
my cats leaping out of nowhere like UFOs.

BAD HABITS

BAD HABITS

(after "Top Eleven Bad Habits of Shooters," www.bullseyepistol.com)

Aiming at happiness destroys it.
Kant

i Not Looking at the Sights

> *This quite frequently is listed as "looking at the target." A shooter*
> *may be focusing his eye on neither the sights nor the target, but since*
> *he does not see the target in clear focus he assumes he is looking at*
> *the sights.*

First frost, heart as dopey as the spiders
outside his window, oozing rather than spinning,
an indulgence of legs just squatting there,
overcome with both real and imagined cold.

He has fate right there in his sights: yellow-
grey skies like blonde hair on its way to white,
trees that couldn't look deader if they up and died,
and those spiders, husks really, hunched in what
used to be called a breeze but is now a wind.
"Remember," he says to me, "when you wrote
November is the beginning of the end?"
Only bastards put misery in italics.

Surely there's something good to focus on,
I almost say, all the coldness getting
to me, stunning me stupid. What about
that Yellow Brick Road of leaves on the lawn?
What about squirrels with Dizzy Gillespie cheeks?

> And what about herself, the one who might invent
> a miracle and rescue the both of us, the one whose
> heart is as playful and resilient as a polar bear?

He takes another drag on his wrinkled cigarette

and aims a finger at his head. "In your dreams,"
meaning me, not him, crazy, not dead.

If only I could fall asleep in a field of licorice
and let the snow just sugar me.
If only I could borrow a set of spider legs
and dash in every direction at once.
I'm trying to look at the bright side,
but all I see is smoke, feel the slap of
unhappiness as it tears itself from his icy chest.

How quickly I'm reduced to magic,
sawing God into halves of halves.
Be happy, you Capricorn, you Catholic,
you Inner Child. I want to snatch his cigarette
and burn a ruby on his wrist, spread his lips
into the dawning realization of a smile.

I want to show him where a secret window might be,
glass so clean it tastes of glaciers,
with busy silver spiders adding shimmer
like sparkles on Shania's gown.

I want him to surrender, like sex,
to the vision of it all, heart swelling,
target coming closer and closer.
Smoke hangs mid-air, a spiderweb.
Look, right there, one flimsy strand,
a man's hopes and dreams, a dare.

Anything less than this is subsistence:
November nosing grit across the frozen ground,
yellow leaves like wings the frost has shot down.

ii Holding Too Long

Any adverse conditions that interrupt a shooter's ability
to "hold" will cause him to delay his squeeze, waiting for
conditions to better. The disturbing factor about this is
that you will do it unconsciously; therefore, you must
continuously ask yourself, am I being too particular?

Demerara sugar in his tea, a crate of clementines
on the kitchen table, radio dialled only to CBC.
Good taste, good health, misery deserves the best.

"He emitted a sound like laughter," but it was never
the kind of laughter that bubbled from a pink spot
at the back of his throat and tickled on its way up his tongue.
It was bitter, esophageal, as if happiness
was choking on a meal of chicken bones.

Aiming for paradise, hitting Pretoria, his lot in life.
He showers, he dreams, he dresses, he
hesitates, happiness always a verb or two out of reach.

The tinkle of spoon in tea is almost art, the room
otherwise hushed, a spray of orange peels
in the shape of Italy. A gorgeous gloom.

How he longs for a simpler language, where every
vowel aches with regret. "I" in particular,
the blue pang of a held back breath.

iii Improper Grip or Position

Suffice to say that you cannot fire a decent score with any gun at any
range if you continually change your grip or position.

The first time he's revived, he starts watching
late night evangelists. It's just him and the Man from God.
Even Letterman is snoring.

This is followed by a semblance of angels and aliens,
something to do with the Northern Lights and too much nicotine.

Anything less than this is subsistence: a temporary score
with an early mass on *Vision*, then an *A.M. Canada*
piece on Mackenzie King's creaky ghost.
Finally, sleep deprived, *Sally* or *Maury*
or *Montel* chanting small doses of self-help.

Triggered, a scattershot swallow of the sweetest-looking pills.
Once again, survives, firing all his faith at therapy,
a German Dr. who says "Calm down" just the way he likes.

Of course, little stony side trips along the way,
everything from bennies to whores.

And then the pineapple diet. The Buddhist retreat.
The life-altering trip to Montreal.

The last of his 9 lives, he grips and aims a hot blue flame
at poetry, collecting titles for books he hasn't written yet.
Finally breathing out.

He emits a sound like laughter, the way God guffaws
as an earthquake, all the rocks rolling from their bored little lives.

Suffice to say, what about herself, thoughts and phrases jumbling
like crazy. *Surely there's something good to focus on.*
He makes a Henry the VIIIth fist and brings it down hard
on the table. Misery scatters, then settles like dust.

iv Jerk or Heel

The application of pressure either with the trigger finger alone or
in case of the heel, pushing with the heel of the hand at the same
time. Apply pressure to the trigger straight to the rear and wait for
the shot to break.

Jerk or heel? Live or die? The jack of spades looks
perplexed, hell, we all do, page boys just a bit
too perfect, that glaze of *what the fuck?*

You can probably feel the pressure for yourself, the way
heat builds after a day of Hawaiian sun.
Being human is another way of saying *boom*:
unhappy. But that's him talking now, again.
Squeezing my wrist, penmanship wonky.
Why are the wrong words always so much easier to say?

How about *we*? We are all heels – the poet,
the German Dr., the suicidal man smoking spiderwebs,
the jack of hearts you feel you've earned
with your willingness to listen. We are all dying
unhappily. All broken long before the end.

And hoping – the amazing phoenix
with an Arabian desert's worth of ashes
pouring from its wings. We are all found
hoping at the strangest moments, hearts aflame.
His kitchen table, my computer desk,
the entire globe, engrossed in clouds of smoke.

Live another day, that old-time revealed religion.
If the penny lands on its head   if an orgy of lucky numbers
if the dream contains both a fish and a naked body. Today,
I feel like the jack of diamonds and that's more than enough.

Tomorrow, I'll be a jerk again, and he'll still be dead,
after a meagre stipend of better days

gambled in the dark. And what are your plans,
my brave heel of the hand? *Calm down*, just the way we like.

I want to show you where a secret window might be,
where the glass has been blown out, the pressure
smashed, the smoke dispersing, the air breathing itself again.

v Anticipation

Anticipation can cause muscular reflexes of an instant nature that so
closely coincide with recoil that extreme difficulty is experienced in
making an accurate call. Anticipation is also the sire to flinching.

The small silver dessert spoon
with the grape vine design on its handle
taunts him the entire time he's chawing on prime rib.

Anticipation, freak tyranny. He might as well be
gnawing on a dinosaur bone. Tasting into the future,
flinching as each second holds its breath.

Time itself corrupt, the past five minutes
dead as a slab of meat. And the stink
of five minutes before that.

Tonight, he feels like one big muscle reflex,
improvident, impossible to please. Lurching
towards the scent of sugar, the next grand tease.

If only I could fall asleep in a field of licorice.
Recoil, the same awful dream: dying
with an empty ice cream scoop in his mouth.

Finally, bones cleared away, a shush of
dabbing napkins. How something so oozy
and caramel could be so accurate –
the mystery overwhelms.

Perfect, for an instant, until the last taste
reminds him of the taste before
and he begins to think ahead to coffee
with its cheering undertow of cream.
Oh, next best thing! Keep sifting through the cutlery.
He can always eat his own fingers along with crumbs.

vi Loss of Concentration

> *If the shooter fails in his determination to apply positive pressure*
> *on the trigger while concentrating on the front sight his prior*
> *determination needs renewal and he should rest and start over.*

Mooning about in bed, almost noon, concentrating
on the spank his feet will make when they land on the floor.
Just a little positive pressure.
But then a vision of herself intrudes
and he forgets all about his real body.

In the vision, his blood's gone hard
and he's sucking on a hot part of her neck.
While she's spraying kisses like champagne.
Pure bliss, until a sudden flicker of worry
(a cat left out or an unpaid Hydro bill)
replaces his unreal self with yet another version.

The amazing phoenix... calling "Kitty, Kitty,"
as he fumbles through the dark, wondering
where herself has gone, all their determination,
boom: gone up in smoke.

> Rest, retrain, he spends another day in bed,
> selves all over the place.

vii Anxiety

You work and work on a shot, meanwhile building up in your
mind doubt about the shot being good.

He resolves to adopt a plan composed of discipline,
diligence and courage. Work and more work,
sweating his way to happiness.

November though is full of doubt, all its measly slaves
shuffling in the gutters, unable to tell the difference
between death and sleep. No wonder
his left hand shakes like the last brown leaf on a tree.
He takes up jogging, filling the empty streets
with his formerly useless feet.

The way heat builds after a day of Hawaiian sun,
so do those flare-ups of inner strength, until it feels
as if his muscles are burning consciousness.

"Just get rid of it!" The one point, the only point.
He's not even looking when he hits that gnarled hedge,
ass over elbows, skinning himself across a yard and a half.

Instantaneous anxiety, his mind building chills,
spreading from the tips of his scraped toes
all the way to his bald spot. Wishes he could
just blend in, the sky mistaking him for a bone.

And then he builds some more: a little burial mound
of humiliation he can wear on his head. Stick by stick,
he self-disciplines, boldly hating his every thought.
It's all work, isn't it, the fucking up, the dropping dead?

viii Vacillation (Plain Laziness)

This is a mental fault more than a physical one, which results in your
accepting minor imperfections in your performance which you could
correct if you worked a little harder. The end result being you hope you
get a good shot.

"We're all concoctions," I explain.
Minor imperfections, sure. But attributes too,
like the way he shares the cream, even at a trickle,
or the time he snuck me cigarettes when I had my tonsils out.

And then there's all the stuff he'd like to be:
better looking, atomic talking, worry-free,
able to fly. Parts of him, if only.

"You're a fucking inflorescence," is what I say
when I want to go too far.

The way heat builds after a day of Hawaiian sun
is the way you love someone
who can't live with or without happiness.
(I know he's getting close when I start talking about you.)
One explosion of hope after another.

He disagrees, of course, his worst habit.
When he stares in the mirror, all he can see
is his stupid desire to be handsome.
He worries about not being worry-free.

A strange kind of predatory pricing, finally less
than a loonie. He flips an easy penny in the air
and calls, "Whatever's in between."

Instead of working harder, he sinks lightly into gratis dreams:
a small inheritance from a previously unknown uncle in Transylvania,

a night on the town with Lois Lane, a brain transplant
involving Einstein and one of the actors from *ER*.

There is no correct way to say, "You blew it."
The strain of frequent imperfection thins the skin
around what used to be his smile.
When he sucks on a cigarette, it looks
like he's trying to swallow his face.
His ears are red and twisted. His eyes
an empty parking space.

"We're all missing pieces," I venture,
the gap between my two front teeth
producing an inappropriate whistle. Best we can do
is incomplete. No matter how much
I'd like to be a hyphen, a knot, a relationship.

"You're an end result," is all I can think of to say.

ix Lack of Follow Through

*Follow through is the subconscious attempt to keep everything just
as it was at the time the shot broke. In other words you are
continuing to fire the shot even after it is gone.*

What a footslog, from the dreary parking lot
to the falsely cheery lobby
where old women in bright yellow jackets
give directions to Psych, calling me "Dear"
half a dozen times. Follow through, one heartbeat
after another. The elevator rises like a last expectation.
He downs me at the door with drug-shot eyes.

We talk self-consciously while an overhead TV
plays born-again Christians on mute. We don't mention
the plural for diazepam. We pretend not to notice
where the wild-haired girl across the room is putting her fingers.

Might as well be on the moon: *Nice view, eh?*
Nurses float down the halls, having given up on
gravity long ago. "It's a beautiful day out there,"
I lie, "for November." Ah, sweet stupor.
He doesn't even worry why the walls are painted orange
when everyone else knows orange is not a calming colour.

A strange kind of predatory pricing, this two-bit visit,
this low level sit and stare. In other words
I am bigger than a pill bottle but nowhere near
as skilled. My only hope is a pair of *Reeboks*
with the feeble smell of November on their laces.

x Lack of Rhythm

> *Hesitancy on the first shot or any subsequent shot in timed or
> rapid fire. Develop a good rhythm and then have the fortitude to
> employ it every case.*

A crow lands on the just-snowed oak in a flourish
of black hesitation, a blip in a skyful of flight plans.
He matches the indecision from his perch on the bed,
toes two inches from the cold rug. Good rhythm,
good riddance, another dangerous morning.

Today the list of imponderables is longer than
any wingspan. He's caught in a pause between
More snow? and *Calm down,* all intentions gone mad.
Even the air feels tangled, crow's feet tied up in knots.

Fortitude, a voice from the past, some teacher
or maiden aunt. He listens, but that's all he can do.
He has always listened. A blow of snow
against the window, *the beginning of the end* again.
A caw as the oak tree clutches its roots.

Finally, he manages a lurch. Stumbles his way
to the even colder bathroom, his eyes crashing

into the mirror. There has to be a pill to fill this
emptiness, and another one to kill the pain.

Christmas is coming, he says out loud, hoping
for a plastic thrill. Something to aim for?
He twists on the tap and before he knows it,
starts swallowing, the blues first, followed
by the kiwi greens, saving just a handful in case
the crow is still there when he trips back to bed.

The jack of spades looks perplexed. It's snowing
hard now, too hard to identify anything on a branch.
Impossible for an ambulance to read the numbers
on his house. He considers cawing,
but *emits a sound like laughter* instead.

Nearly man for a moment more, then a flourish
of nothing (yes, nothing can do whatever it pleases).
A blue bit of drool crawling across the pillow case.

xi Match Pressure

*If there are 200 competitors in a match, rest assured that there are
200 shooters suffering from match pressure. So what makes you
think you are so different?*

There are at least 200 graves surrounding his grave,
lots of holy lettering: *Gone*
But Not Forgotten and *In The Arms*
Of God. That and grass, a minimalist's dream.

Tears have drained from my face, lips bit all the way
to blood. Where are the 200 other mourners
like myself, chewing on their leavings of rage?
Together, we could rip wreaths
apart, lop the heads off angels.

Crows splitting their wings in fury, spiders
shredding their immoderate legs, bitter
secretions soaking into the hard green earth.

Hoping for a plastic thrill, I fill my brain with thoughts
of afterlife, a 12-foot Jesus, a soft sad cloud,
a celestial shooting match, something to support
the weight of all this absence.

Who knew nothingness was such a team effort:
200 ghosts with blood dripping from their invisible arms
as they aim my heart back between my ribs.
He's somewhere in the fray, I'm sure, complaining
of sore spirits, wishing he could be the one to get inside my chest.

This is the last of us, the city limits. It's you, or you,
or you, from here on in. Hanging with your family,
hitting the same high notes as the crowd, helping
a stranger cross a street, hoping to be happy
in the process. All through November...
What makes you think you are so alone?

PLURAL

Christ had his 12 disciples, Kurosawa his 7 Samurai.
My wife and I can sometimes get as high as 5 or 6,
our parents, even the dead ones, still up to their tricks.

Constellations of us, never really alone, not with our inner guides,
our good memories, our greatest hits radio stations
playing *We Are Family* for the zillionth time.

And my cousin, the one who hung himself in his cell
at Penetang, was it a simple split personality
or a goddamn parliament of voices colliding in his head?

To be has never felt so plural, everything from
kindred souls to angels of death, from *you're always
in my thoughts* to *I will forgive,*

but not forget. Christ crying in all those churches,
warriors shouting at one another through the common language
of mud and blood. Couples saying the same things

over and over again. Even the worst silence,
the lack of sound after the last sound, is left hanging
there, invisible feet just inches off the ground.

THERE ARE MOODS

There are moods when the world suddenly
    sucks itself small,
a dead man's *House and Home,*
the colour taupe unconscious on the walls,
    objets d'art shrinking beauty,
IKEA carpet like an Abba song, undressed.

Such a tenuous state, something a
    cigarette might feel.
Life is short and yet, that brevity
drags on and on. You look in the mirror and see
    taupe eyes surveying taupe skin.
You sense your own bones shrinking.

Try spotting the plasma in a drop of blood
    or trapping the soul
in a handshake. Small and tight,
meaning eludes you. There are moods
when you can barely
find a place to disappear.

How easily the mind can be reduced
    to a single-celled organism,
a simple algae creeping across the room,
an amoeba of a womb giving birth to misery.
    Feel yourself squirming,
aching for a speck of beauty.

There are moods when the pain of being alive
    is skin and bone,
the mansions in your father's realm the size of
Monopoly houses. Listen to those threadbare
    songs, those shrinkings,
the dead man within so close you can feel his lack of breath.

TAKING CARE

An entire morning attached to my
central vac, the dustball hunter, I drag
the tuberous hose from room to room.
Hardly high on the theological
scale of things. What am I living for?
A bucket of *Mr. Clean,* a can
of *Comet,* a duster made from
a yellowing pair of *Fruit of the Looms.*

Once I was kept alive by lilacs,
their sweet stink overpowering
my GI Joe's of pain. How many times
have lily of the valley encouraged me
to take another breath? Isn't that
the way it is in movies:
Woody Allen suddenly stripped of
his puniness by a Gershwin blossom?

Now I raise my arms to celebrate
a cobweb dangling from the ceiling.
Eureka, my heartfelt response as
tea stains are bleached from the kitchen sink.
Don't get me started on toilet bowls,
all that swirling water, south-seas blue.
In the name of everything clean, why
didn't Sylvia Plath just scrub that oven,
find solace in its temporary gleam?

Some days I stay alive to trim the ficus,
to trudge through the litter box with my
slotted spoon, to wash the Romanian
crystal candlestick and think of Bucharest
in the spring. If only Virginia Woolf
hadn't been able to afford servants.
If only my cousin could have hung orchids
or model airplanes in his Penetang cell.

Every now and again taking care is
as holy as you can muster, stroking
the bathroom tiles with a soft, wet sponge,
nestling leftover pasta in *Tupperware*
bowls, kissing Anne Sexton's *Selected*
before slipping it back on the shelf.

FOUR THINGS TO CONSIDER BEFORE COMMITTING SUICIDE

i Crashing

Lift-off is the hardest part,
whether knees are buoyant enough,
trigger fingers flexible,
stomachs strong. How deeply
can you breathe? Can't be afraid
of heights, or the sight of blood,
or swallowing huge handfuls of pills.
For once in your life, you have to be sure.

No more bouquets of bacon and coffee.
Say goodbye to Ruby Braff and tulip
trees and blow jobs. Let go of
all those revised opinions, vacation plans,
your scheme to build a gazebo out
by the blue spruce. To exist is an entire language,
whittled down to a final word like *shoot*
                   or *jump*.
Where you're going, Bibles shudder
before leaping back into motel drawers.
Cheating's out, no telephone numbers
written on your wrist, no kiss to
sip on like a sugar cube.

Isn't there a better way of reprimanding the world?
A harsh frown, perhaps, a scream?
Hang loose, my love, breathe easy, boy,
crash awhile in the arms of doubt.

ii Truthless

Truth has very few friends and those few are suicides.
Antonio Porchia

What makes you think death will be less claustrophobic
than your own two arms? Can peace
really be the booby prize? Picture yourself,
an implosion on the tip of a bullet,
a kaleidoscope of oxygen-starved dreams.
A body splat on the sidewalk, stains for weeks.
Hanging gardens of blue, swollen truths.

Don't waste a wish on heaven, its fabled
golden bricks. Like Scheherezade,
you'll be sleepless inventing 1,001 excuses.
And God is going to choke up
as He listens to the one about your brain breaking
on the same day as your best friend fled
and the stranger in the tan *Tercel* gave you the finger.

iii They Love You

She loves you, way beyond her fear of
abandonment, her preference for perfection.
He loves you deeper and dizzier
than men are supposed to love.

Look at her, waving as your car slides
down the driveway, just wanting to be
visible, your last glimpse of love.
What you can't see are his hands
holding each other behind his back.
You can't even imagine the kitchen chair
longing for your thighs, the pink pillowcase
displaying one of your hairs, the mauve shirt

calling from its stack of others,
softly seductive at the neck and wrists.

Not to mention the love of your own body,
ripples, fuzz, earlobes begging to be stroked.
Your ligaments, freckles, capillaries,
                endearments
whispered to your blood. Nothing more faithful
than ankles, more devoted than thumbs.
Your penis at attention, extra inches
loud, gushing over with sheer delight.

iv Missing

Have you any idea how much I'll miss you?
This will be a poem without tremors,
a ghost stripped of its white sheet.
In the middle of my tears for Madame Bovary
and the entire Buendia clan, another torrent,
a terrible sob torn from the soreness of my throat.
I will keep adding syllables to the loss of you,
deeper and deeper holes.

I am beginning to feel like a parasite, feeding off
the imagined cold of your long, sad sleep. There are
days when my mouth hangs open, flies building
blue castles in the spaces between my teeth.
There are dreams where my body is breaking, remorse
bled of all its grace. Still, I can't forget you,
the revolving red light in your frightened eyes,
the twist in your tongue tying knots
in even simple words like *and* and *then*.

Think about this, wherever you find yourself.
Missing the idea of you, my love.
The split second of a last breath.
If we could only talk awhile, untangle
the mysterious lack of everything.

SOCRATES THE CATERPILLAR

Is there really anything worth dying for?
asked the tattered ant
after witnessing thousands of her family
crushed while exercising their right
to build hills in the grassy forests.
Is freedom absolutely necessary?
cried the tiny red spider
as he spun his doomed web
across the giant's dining room.
Scores of moths piously setting fire
to themselves.
And all those homeless houseflies,
drunkenly devoted to the beauty in everything,
slapped and sprayed and squashed.
Is just being alive a form of suicide?
queried Socrates the caterpillar,
barely escaping a rain of kerosene
poured over his brother's fluffy nest.
To thine own self be true, muttered Shakespeare
the praying mantis, who never struck a pose
or nibbled on a mate
without believing it was the correct thing to do.
So what are the rewards of this precious virtue?
The air thick with all kinds of kamikaze angels,
ghosts of former royalty,
remnants of evolution's miracles.
Creatures who died for natural causes:
honey siphoned from a hive, pretty
rigor mortis pinned to a board, belly
dances on the end of a hook.
No wonder the stoned white grub
just squats there, pretending to be
nothing more than an albino clump of dirt.
And who can blame the fleas
for making their bloodlust so miniscule
they can't even see themselves.
Is dying worth living for? asked Socrates,

the entire insect world stubbornly holding its breath,
a dead silence followed by
so much buzzing, clacking and whirring
that it sounded as if the world
was being created all over again.

SHRIEK

What is this shriek that lifts me from my chair
and to the window? And raises the hair
on the back of my neck? I expect to
find a body hanging from the oak tree,
but all I can see is a bummed robin
staring down a black cat, and I can't decide
which one would shriek. Maybe it's the 40,000
oak leaves, the tree shuddering at the thought
of tensed muscles or drawn claws.
Or perhaps the robin's mate squealing in
the empty air above the tree, stripping
gears switching its brain from *safe* to *slaughter*.
Even the air itself sweeping flesh and
feather and all those molecules of
cowardice into a climax of dread.
I can feel my own little Icarus
screech clawing at the bottom of my throat,
all those dark possibilities. Or is
it God deep inside us all opening
his deep black hole and screaming fear and
fear alone? For now, the scene is silent
as a still life: acorn-studded grass, cat's
frozen green eyes, robin's fan-like tail feathers
just hanging there. But what if I continued
to listen, wouldn't a twig or a cloud
eventually give itself up with a cry?
There's a ton of terror out the window, too much
for one small beak, one tiny set of jaws.
The shriek of gravity cracking and tearing
as balance falls completely out of sight.

RECOGNITION

I recognize him by the rope burn
he wears around his blue, swollen neck.
The lips that press against his cheekbone
belong to his mother. And the fingertip
that barely touches one patch of raw
                           below his ear
is the best his father can do. The others,
blushing at how much they care, are sisters
and cousins, who stand in the background
like bad news, the tightness of their own
collars creating tiny rasps of breath.

When I can't bear to look at him anymore,
I can still feel the bulk of that rope
weighing us down. I can picture him
dangling in the middle of his cell,
the swing of him like a long wave goodbye.
How can we shoulder such a burden?
The words he never whispered in my ear
are heavy like buckets of soaking wet sand.
Imagine a lifetime's worth of apologies
and explanations. It's my own weight
                          against the coffin
that threatens to tip the day, but it feels
like his body pressing against mine.

To get further away, I try those
memory stunts where fantasy rushes in
to save the day. But all I can conjure
are real moments, fragments of intimacy
flung out across the years. That night when
I held his hair back as the combination
of rum and sadness flowed into the sink,
surprised at the soft, baby-like dampness
of his forehead. Or a more philosophical
evening, sharing stories and cigarettes
on the picnic bench, his smoke coming out
of my lungs. Or that last day when I dipped

a hand into the pocket of his frayed brown coat
and found his fingers there amidst the coins
and lint, holding them for just a moment
before muttering *Sorry* and pretending
                    to be alone again.

Soon, the rope burn and the powder barely
camouflaging his blue face will be buried
along with the rest of him. I'll dream about
him for awhile, hearts bursting mid-air
like crazed pinatas, until one day grief
will trickle into blue basins like
a royal dynasty's final drops of blood
and I'll forget for stretches at a time
that he was here and gone, that once his death
ruled my every vision. For now, I share
his absence, I curl a phantom of his hair
between my fingers, I fall into
an empty pocket and stay there for days.
Between these moments, I recognize
myself, a stranger to everyone but him.

EVERYWHERE

It was dawn, pink-whiskered,
when I saw the sleepy school
of perch bobbing your severed head
across the bay. Then later,
nearly noon, a swirl of glossy
ants brandishing what looked like
your baby finger up the beach.

Just as I feared: you're everywhere,
blushing in a blur of sumacs,
dangling from the beak of
a bad-boy crow, whistling
through the perfect lips of the wind.
Absence is a synonym
for infinite. Last evening,
silver-plated, the moon grinned your grin.

It was midnight when I
finally saw the whole of you
beside me on the bed.
Black-eyed, you were lifting
the sheets of my skin,
staring holes into my bones.

THE SANGRE DE CRISTO CLOSED ROAD BLUES

It was on the plane to Albuquerque
when the flimsiest of clouds suddenly decided

to form the shape of a semicolon, a pause
between countries perhaps, or the shift in clauses

between *before you* and *after the fact*,
even though you had nothing at all to do with the trip,

part holiday, part D.H. Lawrence trek,
to the ranch in the Sangre de Cristo Mountains

(imagine Anglos naming anything the Blood of
Christ except a cocktail), ironic,

since neither you nor Lorenzo were believers,
except in the faith of your own blood

as it seared through your able veins,
which is as close to a full stop as I care to come,

one of those periods so black it looks like a chasm
at the end of the last sentence in the universe,

an apt way to describe that road
twisting into the mountains just outside of Taos

where our rented *Dodge Aries*,
as white a chariot as *Avis* could conjure,

grumbled its way around a ROAD CLOSED sign,
steering for the climb, me keeping one eye

on the ever-rising clouds, searching for an exclamation point,
something to mark the occasion, finally

getting to meet Lawrence's hallowed bones
in that chapel hanging on the side of a hill,

filled with love notes from other obsessives,
some of whom had come a much longer flight than me,

bringing their own shaky ghosts, lost ones like you
whose passion for death had caused the sky to pause,

and loved ones to scatter their broken hearts
over the bumpy heights of the past, a place

where Lawrence praised the aspens
and began writing poetry again, no wonder

the woods looked so holy, sunlight streaming
through thin leaves, and the rocks like cemetery stones,

moss-eaten names only a psychic could read,
the kind of messages writers like to plant in books,

surprising future generations with their wisdom
and how, in the end, it didn't come close to saving them,

or you, who loved both the purple passages
and the declarations of philosophy, who agreed

that life was blood, was lust, and had to be obeyed,
even when it burned in pain, when the body cried out

to stop all this nonsense, fling open the parentheses,
toss the commas with their cautious little steps,

scrawl your way to the bottom of the page,
the great THE END, which is exactly where I found myself,

at the closure of what had once been Lawrence's driveway,
being scalded by a groundsman who skinned me

with questions like, *Can't you read?*, shouting about forest fires
and tourists with their careless passions, *Okay,*

Of Course, but did ROAD CLOSED mean obsessions put aside,
a cowardly flight back to Toronto where the roads whistled

with your absence, cars full of strangers who couldn't
have cared less about anyone's blood but their own,

I think not, so I stood there, stubborn as no words at all,
and uttered *PLEASE*, then a softer repetition, more plea

than demand, an ellipsis that I hoped would lead
to the chapel, to Lawrence's bloody presence, and maybe

even a momentary sound bite of you reading the first poem
in *Look! We Have Come Through!*, ah, what I was waiting for,

an exclamation point, two of them, Lawrence's blessing
lifting me through the lofty pines, to the very spot in the sky

where you've chosen to spend your eternity, doing tricks
with clouds, and road signs, making sure all my travels

end in the same sad question mark, back down that road again,
chapel-less, alone, dumbfounded so much distance

can result in so little resolve, just that fish hook of punctuation
holding the entire Sangre de Cristo range in place,

the same shape my heart takes when, torn
and disgruntled, it dangles in what feels like outer space;

THE CROWD OF HIM

FATHER-LOVE

Self-possessed, sufficient, my father
lives his real life in the driveway
flat on his back, sinking into
the soft sun-warmed asphalt
an angel spilled from a black hole.
He is puddle life, a collision
of grease and DNA
crawling out from underneath
the rusty crust of a car
wrenches poking from his bald fists
an unexpected smile twisting
his lips, teeth exposed like bones.

Flesh melded to metal, this is
what his love must feel like.
The way he polishes spark plugs
whispers *piston* and *camshaft*
shows the fan belt exactly where to go.
With his breath he buffs the headlights.
Reveres the rearview mirror.
Wipes the windshield
with an old pair of underwear.

Discreet and patient, I imagine
he often waits for my childhood
curiosity to fall asleep
then invites my mother
to join him, just a moment or two
the backseat of his old *Dodge*
roomy and spotless.
Ah, the weekly love affairs
on *Route 66*.
The magic of *clutch*
and *dimmer switch*.
It is these dark moments my mother
is faithful to, the moon squeezed

between the houses, no bigger
than a flashlight beam.

Come look
says the secret father
to his spying son
as I step over smears of grease
careful not to disturb a tool.
I stand there, staring down at him
through spaces in the engine
loving a button, a kneecap
a black vein on his wrist, wishing
he would invite me to lie beside him
hand me a cap or a valve
something to make a perfect fit.

PRETENDING

My fury with my father
is 46 years old today.
It blows a whistle, its squadron
of insecurities and rages
instantly snapping to attention
like a West Point drill.
It marches out into the suburbs,
stopping for no-one, trampling
postcard lawns and beds of pansies,
yells *Attack!* at the first sight
of that yellow bungalow,
my father sitting on the porch
blatant as a bull's eye,
pretending to be old and frail.

My wife intrudes
just before the execution.
Daydreaming again?
She sips a wine spritzer,
relaxing on a sunny chair
as if our house were somewhere
in the south of France.
I snap, or maybe shout – exactly
my father's strategy
for shutting everyone out –
castle doors clanging in all directions.
And then I'm angry
with myself, whirling around,
a bullet hole straight through my heart.

Visiting my father, I feel
like one of those ghosts
condemned to the house it died in,
trailing its gruesome rosary of chains –
pain and boredom, boredom and pain.
You never loved me praised me
taught me how to believe
a woeful bellyache

aeons below words.
Sitting side by side on the couch
my father and I chat about Mike Harris
or the new *Toyotas*, assuming
nonchalance or memory loss,
pretending we can walk through walls.

DISAPPEARING FATHERS

What do we do about our disappearing fathers
whose Florida tans are blanched
by that first sign of trouble?
A cough, a weak spell,
a won't-go-away shiver,
and the man (*the* man)
squelched to a whimper,

a slit of animal eyes
burning through the dark.
The ambulance rush, the apt wail,
our doom wheeled into *Emergency*
where the sweat and glare
remind us of a laundromat.
Crowds are always a surprise,

we're usually so alone.
We never realized how death
will multiply our fathers,
rooms full of shadows writhing on blank walls.
Of all my sums and sins
I am most guilty of sleeping away
a dreary Sunday afternoon,

missing an instant of memory
as my father edged closer to death.
In the end all I can recall
are the big occasions:
the colour of his knuckles
as he hoisted his own father's coffin,
the tumble of his limbs

as he tripped over our sneaky Persian,
toppling feet first down the stairs,
the way his eyelids wrinkled
as they wheeled him out of the recovery room.
These are the only facts

that will outlive my father,
a string too short

to fit around my neck.
Where do our fathers go
once they've been given back?
Our father, who art in absentia.
In *Births and Deaths* 16 men died today:
the father of my father of my father.
We haven't a clue

how to fight for their lives.
My best friend's father treading
the water in his lungs,
my father-in-law betrayed by his own liver.
More disappearances each year:
old men last seen in hospital halls
like statues of obsolete saints.

WINGS

My father thinks the backyard birds
perform for him alone, as if the sky
were a sheet strung between trees on which
a 1960's family watched home movies.
Geez, those Speedy Gonzalez hummingbirds, that
cardinal done up like a harlot, and what about
the yellow finch shitting its way across the roses,
a real fireworks. But it's the measly
robin he falls in love with, the one that splashes
in the grass, Midas in a heap of golden worms.
She sat in my lap just a minute ago, he
swears, *wings beating like a pair of draped open hearts.*
And I can feel the skitter, the flick, flick, flick
of her love on my own skin, just an instant of
belonging, of being more to the world than
a hoe and rake, a measly man. Do I long
for the embrace of senility? A blue jay bursting
from the brain behind my eyes, double-dipping
itself in sunlight, asking me to spread my arms.

ENLIGHTENED

A frenzied pounding at the back door, my
father's eyes grey with shock. *I've shit myself.*
Forgot his key in the left pocket, not the right.
For one enlightened moment, I forgot
everything as well, reduced to an urge to
hit him, watch him splatter against the door.
I bet Christ never soiled his robes,
and Buddha wouldn't care once he'd
emptied his mind of human thoughts.
There's a whole town of people out there
with enough sense to hide their bodily functions.
Even the dogs wear tiny plastic bags
hanging from their tails. But there's my father,
reeking openly, lost in vast dimensions of
shame, asking more of me than I'd ever planned to
give. Was it love when I helped him undress,
when I piled his clothes in the washing machine,
when I sat in a deck chair and scrubbed
the shit from his shoelaces? What was it
that made me finally realize how small
I was inside, beyond the emptiness,
the wall of fists, the inconvenience of feelings?

WHERE?

You threw your life away, all 88 years,
    the hospital a dumping ground for sprung bones
and leaky stuffing. For what, and where? Should I
    be picturing you in Caracas, a puff
of white sand? Or maybe the moon, a braggart's
    grin? Wherever you are, you're fiddling with that
light bulb in my brain, off and on, again, again.

If only you'd stuck around, more legendary.
    I could have propped you at the kitchen table,
a lazy Susan of small wisdoms. My father,
    Methuselah of my heart. 89, 90, staying
power, showing off his late life love. 96, 97,
    like a tower of pennies defying gravity.
Imagine 100, now that takes balls, Roman candles
    blistering the sky. We could have walked
into the horizon together, bones on bones.

But you threw me away along with sunsets
    and macaroni, the world
nothing more than a piddling fish.
    Going on alone,
wondering whether my prize-winning poem
    was a wink from the great beyond,
or just a momentary happy feeling, a postcard
    from Pleasantville. Is it okay
if I imagine you gleaming in Giza, whispering
    in a sphinx's ear, the secret formula for
eternity? Now *that* would be a souvenir.

MISSING PERSON

I've rifled every pocket
he ever fingered, roamed through
his desk with a magnifying glass.
Buttonholes and bank codes
only pretend to be human;
an instant after you're gone
they're emptiness and arithmetic.

I've frisked photo albums, closet
shelves, tool chests, searched matchboxes,
golf bags, tobacco pouches,
all his theatrical props.
I've even raged under
a full moon, shovelling sweat,
discovering bones all look alike.
In the flicker of home movies,
he already resembles
a ghost. But then so do I,
a 10-year-old boy long
put away, like the smallest
in a set of Russian dolls.

And so I start digging in
my own heart, the grave my feelings
have become. Finally, roiling
at the core, there he is – my father –
a muddy swirl of dead. *Keepsakes
are for fools*, he says, having shed
possessions with a shrug. His only
remaining desire is that
I close my eyes and count to ten,
time enough for him to untie
the red knot of my love and
disappear for good. Grief, an empty
urn on the mantelpiece
between the photos of him
disguised as a shirt and a smile.

THE CROWD OF HIM

Six months dead doesn't stop my father
from sitting smack dab in the middle of the garden,
slouched in the blonde Muskoka chair, dwarfed
by sweet bergamot and Russian thistle, saying,
Look at that! over and over: hummingbirds,
butterflies, bumblebees, whatever flits by. His,
everything suddenly his, beauty rolled in an eyeball.
Nothing like absence to fill the brain with blossoms
and old man's breath. He sits there
in the weediest part of my brain, tugging,
begging me to see how pretty his fingers are
now that flesh has finally flowered.

Bring on the shears, the poison, the physicists
with recipes for getting rid of energy. Deadhead
the day, let nothingness flourish. Call it
Empty Garden, even if I have to get down
on my belly and gnaw at each and every stem.
Do it for the earthworms, the ladybugs, the sons
of slither and flutter, all those who hate to be watched.

But then dusk finds me soft again; even
a dandelion can break my heart. My wife strolls
in, smelling of damp grass, carrying a vase
she places in the centre of the kitchen table.
There he is, standing at attention this time,
green and willowy like new growth,
up to his miniature waist in moonlight and stems,
a shred of pink phlox in his hair. *Look at this!*
He points at the blur of my arm as it tries to
erase him. He gestures at the spider crawling
down the glassy slope of his own arm. All him,
every scurry and chill, petals spinning a little as they fall.

One day I'll wake up to find a thousand petals
on the table, each softer than the one beneath.
And in the garden, row upon row of blonde
chairs, an audience of dead fathers

watching caterpillars wriggle from their skins,
coneflowers bristling, a circus net of spiderwebs
billowing across the yard, no chance
for emptiness anymore. My father has never
been so vital, so present. The crowd of him
waves amidst the colours and scents.
Look at you, he says, they say,
mere season, acting as if you own the place.

THE CAT'S MEOW

Colour me orange, my father would say,
his lap a carpet of fur from my Persian cat
who would pin him to the couch for hours,
long after the golf game had been replaced
by an infomercial for no-stick pots and pans.

A kind man, and debonair, according to the cats.
Ariel the Manx claimed him as territory,
peeing on the worn green tiles beside his bed.
It takes a gentleman to surrender.

On trips to the vet, he'd sit in the back seat
beside the cage, cooing, his fingers sliding
between the bars. *And you will know him
by his furriness*. His cracked, froggy meows.

Since his disappearance (no sense naming it,
upsetting the cats), Annie, the Persian, has become
a hermit, while Ariel pees in the front hall,
taking ownership of all who dare to enter.

Even black magic Lorenzo, leader of
the whiskered ones, is stunned, living
under the pine dresser where the scales hide,
silently exclaiming the weight of dust.

Monotonic, our days add up, only to be lost
again, the cats practicing their comas,
a hush of fur on every surface. Grief
grey as a stuffed mouse, the only attention.

And we claim sorrow is a human accomplishment,
a broken heart in a puddle by the door.
This could turn into one of those cat-lover poems,
couldn't it? *Feline superius*. A Roget's purr.

Let the fur fly, get those hisses and yowls
out of our systems, death gnawing
on our bones. My father's lap is
gone, but never empty.

UGLY BONES

Dad and I trudging home through the dark woods, cranky
from our too-long visit with dismal Uncle Don,
sliding our bodies between blackness and its
blotto silhouettes. Suddenly, the air
a flicker of excitement, then another,
lights winking at us from behind dark glasses,
bolder by the second, until it's us who
feel exposed, not the fireflies, our moods lit up
like haunted houses, ghosts and their ugly bones.

Tonight, years later, Dad barely the memory
of a bad mood, the soft clay of my nephew
is fired by the same startling scene, fireflies
poking tiny holes in the invisible
everything. Wide-eyed, can hardly tell
the difference between bug and boy,
all boundaries collapsed in a manic burst of sparks.

In the company of fairies, angels, insects,
call them what I dare, my grief exposed, a black
hole in the midst of me where lightning writes its
ghostly scars. Will I ever learn to be more
than moods and feelings? A man going beyond
his Dad, bones tossed in the flickering air.

THREE LIVES/THREE DEATHS

1/

Last life, no talent for reckless ambition or scissoring snowflakes out of old exams, no desire for long hugs or those bath balls that sizzle in the downpour, no time for playing with clouds or being driven mad by clocks that tock instead of tick, death was a computer sitting on a pair of empty shoulders, sorting facts from impressions, storing moods by categories of time and place. Feel it memorizing you, counting its way through room after room of your choicest disappointments. Plug in, log on, the mouse in your right hand: a ghost in the grand machine.

2/

This life, no good for therapy or running naked down a Hampton's beach, no gift for paper airplanes or Humphrey Bogart impressions, no stamina for credit cards or staying put while everyone else flocks to the front of the church, death is the first thing you think about when stripped of distraction, a peel down the back of your neck, your stomach flipped on its side, your knees bent. Feel it remind you of missed opportunities, a plucked hair, a picked-clean chicken wing. The mind/body connection: *the will rules*, even a cold sore doing what it's told.

3/

Next life, no longer a slave to bones or pens leaking in a pocket, no need for clean clothes or crackers to quell the nausea, no interest at all in program notes or those tiny heaps skunks dig on suburban lawns, death will opt for something fiery, something poured, a thin stream of brandy flowing over a numb dish of ice cream. Feel it scalding your inner corridors, steaming in the happy spot just below your heart. Reach for another spoonful, cold/hot, nerves/feelings, swallow again.

ANGER SONG

On angry days, I sizzle my father
in a wok full of oily red peppers and
onions searing black around the edges.
Serves him right: this meal of grief.

Let's not skimp on negativity,
let's wince at every slight. Feel
abandoned by the air dividing, grumble
over the supercilious nature of death.

And so I feed on gristle and ire, a meal
fit for a masochist. Loss after loss, assembly
line of clock bombs. A human swallowing machine;
the dead keep getting stuck in my throat.

Is it any wonder the words blister
across the page? No surprise when I yell
instead of recite. Father Time and his
Amazing Slaughterhouse, blues for the bellowing.

Living on is so much less than luck and
legwork. Some days it's simply sitting
on the oniony edge of the bed,
lumping it toe by toe, letting it happen.

Beyond this tyranny of mood, I feel
the absence, how ferocious empty space
can be, eating all the strangely naked parts
of me, the tearballs, the lonely cells, the sobs.

I am growing target-fat on all the grief,
stumbling into my 50's like a poked and prodded
bull released from his pen, blinded to everything
but the swirl of the colour red.

Longing to write an ad for *The Grope
and Wail: One dead too many, letting go
fast and cheap.* Creep quietly back to life,
one moment at a time, furtive as a snack.

BAD GUYS

Tony Soprano steaming on a cigar,
my father taking late-life lessons
in greed and homicide, learning how many
humiliating ways there are to thrive or die.
Sitting next to him on the saggy couch,
counting the number of *fucks* per scene,
I can see the pulse skirmishing in his wrist,
a last twinge of innocence, his heart
as blood-stained as a body in a *Caddy*'s trunk.

∞

And he thought De Gaulle was evil.
Hitler, of course.
Men wired into mock Satans by history.
But Tony lives in an actual house,
with cranky kids, and a wife who acts spic and span.
Love thy neighbour? Who's telling this joke?

∞

Senile or simply wised-up, my father swears
my best friend is an impostor, a cold-blooded
bastard who beats him regularly
whenever I'm off at *The West Wing* or *ER*.
Tony morphing from TV set to family room,
sulphur clouds of him, knuckles from head to toe.
Fuck, he booms, from all three mouths.

∞

One night, any night, I suddenly become a killer,
my father's body lying bloody
on the flying carpet beside my bed,
a tiny TV perched on the fringe,

an even tinier version of me
pointing the tiniest smoking gun
at the spot where his heart used to be.
This world of bad guys and their mesmerizing
dreams, where words are one shock
after another, where the morning paper
beats us senseless. A lone soprano
wails in the distance, creepy as a shriek.

I am, he was, we will be,
especially, in love with death.

ALL THESE BODIES

I walk into the chapel in separate parts,
the *Clarks* I bought in Oxford
striding to the coffin, while my *Jack Fraser* arms
grope behind me, desperate for a doorknob,
something to hold me back. My nose aims
for the ceiling: strange naked alliances
with the polar scents of daisies and roses.
Heart digging deeper in my chest.

For a moment, I mistake Uncle Bob's body
for my father's, same solid stillness.
All these bodies, can hardly remember who's
on the guest list and who's already gone.
Cousins sit in the front row, shoes shuffling
in various directions. Who'll be next?

Can't stop thinking about *Disneyworld*'s Hall of
Presidents, its revolving stage of schemers
and heroes, robots all, the skin of their cheeks
scrunched in artificial smiles. Why didn't we
think of propping Bob in a chair, one arm
outstretched, waving. Or my father
leaning against that gaudy purple bouquet,
relishing a last look. The living and the dead
mingle by the bristol board of happy photos,
losing time together. Uncle Ham showing up
year after year like Jerry Lewis and his telethon.

By the skin of their cheeks, how lined we all look
in the florist-lit light, and soft, impressionable.
Neat with our pressed pants and collars.
Cousin Grant folds his fists in front of him, and so do I,
and others, no-one wanting to cry
or rankle. We mimic the dead.

Here I stop being a self, break free
of arms and odours, the whole of me reeling

in the blast of Uncle Bob, all 98 years of his dying.
I hold his hand, welcoming the coldness, touching
my cousins with it, their soft shoulders and elbows.
I even take it home with me, surprising a friend
with a hug, a good, bracing chill. Later,
I will dream about my father and me
sharing the same space in a revolving door.

THE MAN WHO WON'T PLAY POETRY

Opening Rilke at any page, there's my father
convulsing between the lines, the pulse of his
disapproval the only roam of him left alive.
    Is this his rage, or mine? Poetry a waste of
time, especially when the rhymes are breathless,
the similes writing home to make death shine
like fresh-squeezed milk. Blue in the face, he jerks
and shudders, mad dog elegies of foam.

∝

Open all your poetry books, our fathers shooting
    dirty looks, drooling bits of lyric. *My son, the
ballpoint pen(is)*. Even Plath never managed to be so
cruel, that *bastard* seizuring on her fingertips.

And whose thumb is it stuck between Neruda's
    Love Songs despairing how the heart goes soft?
Daddy, is that you, or a leather glove?

∝

Open the rubric of Funeral 101, find all
the places where a poem might apply. *My dad has
graduated to that great image in the sky*. He lies
in sibilance, the fool, his face refusing to bend.

Gunning my father poems, feels more slasher than son.

∝

Opening my head, dad convulsing. *How
    could I? How could I?* the dread of a pulse.
How can one man occupy so many spaces?

He's in the east of me, the west, the least
I can do, the best of my makeshift traces.

∞

Opened, impious, only believing
in what absolutely refuses to die.
My father is scripture in the books I write,
a bite of every word, a long, bloody sip.

Pay attention, the day will come when
the man who won't play poetry is flipped
    on his ribs, shaken by his very tips,
and turned into the one and only poem.

NOTES

"Explicit," stanza 7, "the hammer of red and blue," Wallace Stevens, "The Motive for Metaphor," *The Collected Poems.*

"When the Gods Don't Love You" stanza 1. "Clytie," daughter of Oceanus and Tethys, passionately loved by Apollo. When he deserted her, she was changed into a sunflower, a symbol of faithfulness, devotion, and love.

"Sick Days." The epigraphs are from the following works, listed in the order in which they appear in the poems:
Virginia Woolf, *On Being Ill*
Harriet Martineau, *Life in the Sick-Room*
Rainer Maria Rilke, *Letters to a Young Poet*
John Steffler, title poem, *That Night We Were Ravenous*
"the homely nurse," William Wordsworth, "Ode (Intimations of Immortality...), *The Prelude, Selected Poems and Sonnets*
Edith Wharton, a letter found in R.W.B. Lewis' biography, *Edith Wharton*
Marcel Proust, *Remembrance of Things Past*
Roland Barthes, *A Lover's Discourse*
Katherine Mansfield, *The Journal of Katherine Mansfield*
Aldous Huxley, *Music at Night*
Susan Sontag, *Illness as Metaphor*
Virginia Woolf, *Letters*
Goethe, *Proverbs in Prose*
Donald Westlake, screenplay for *The Grifters*
Elizabeth Philips, "Witness," *A Blue with Blood in It*
Henry Miller, *A Devil in Paradise*
Walter Benjamin, *One-Way Street and Other Writings*
Elias Canetti, *The Secret Heart of the Clock*
Pablo Neruda, "Ode with a Lament," *Selected Poems* (trans. W.S. Merwin)
Flannery O'Connor, *The Habit of Being*

"Bad Habits" is dedicated to the memory of Robert Billings, Mark Matthews and Fraser Jeffrey. The epigraph is from Kant's *Fundamental Principles of the Metaphysics of Morals.*

"Truthless" part ii of "Four Things to Consider Before Committing Suicide." The epigraph is from Antonia Porchia's *Voces*, translated by W.S. Merwin.

ACKNOWLEDGEMENTS

Much appreciation to the editors of the magazines and anthologies where many of these poems first appeared: *The Antigonish Review; CV 2; Danforth Review; Event; Grain; Henry's Creature, Poems and Stories on the Automobile* (Black Moss); *I Want to Be the Poet of Your Kneecaps, Poems of Quirky Romance* (Black Moss); *The Malahat Review; Matrix; The New Quarterly; Prism international; Vintage 95* (Quarry Press); *Wascana Review.*

No matter how many hours spent rearranging the words, I was never completely alone in the process. So many people offered their support and encouragement. Karen Dempster was there in every syllable, with the grace and intelligence to do so much more than just praise. Don McKay, great poet and great editor, was incredibly generous with his boldness, his focus, and his perfect pitch, startling whole sections of this book into shape. Special thanks to Don Domanski for his heart, his wisdom and his always inspiring words. And to Roo Borson for her words as well, and her kindness. Kudos to Kitty Lewis and Maureen Harris who keep the Brick kingdom running so smoothly. And to Glenn Hayes for his good eye and longstanding support. Thanks to Linne Thomson and Linda Gerow, Queen Librarians, who helped so much with the quotes. And for advice, moral support, and frequent illumination, three cheers for Christina & Emilio Aceti, Brian Bartlett, Allan Brown, Katerina Fretwell, Carla Hartsfield, Robert Hilles, Bruce Hunter, Maureen Hynes, Pat Jasper, Penn Kemp, Jacqueline Kolosov-Wenthe, Julia McCarthy, Isabelle Saunders, Naomi Shihab Nye, Sonja Skarstedt, Russell Thornton, Brian, Donna, Kora & Lukas Vanderlip and Liz Zetlin.

Barry Dempster is the author of 8 previous collections of poetry, the most recent being *The Words Wanting Out: Poems Selected and New* (Nightwood Editions). He is also the author of a children's book, two volumes of short stories and a novel, *The Ascension of Jesse Rapture* (Quarry Press). His work has won several distinctions, including a Confederation Poets Prize and a Petra Kenney Award. Born and raised in Toronto, he presently lives 45 minutes north of the city.